CW00545279

FRIES

FRIES

70 crave-worthy recipes from crispy classic to loaded cheese

RYLAND PETERS & SMALL
LONDON • NEW YORK

Designer Paul Stradling
Editor Abi Waters
Head of Production Patricia Harrington
Creative Director Leslie Harrington
Editorial Director Julia Charles

Indexer Vanessa Bird

Published in 2025 by Ryland Peters & Small
20–21 Jockey's Fields
London WC1R 4BW
and
1452 Davis Bugg Road,
Warrenton, NC 27589

www.rylandpeters.com

Text © Valerie Aikman-Smith, Julz Beresford,
Megan Davies, Felipe Fuentes Cruz & Ben Fordham,
Carol Hilker, Jackie Kearney, Jenny Linford, Dan
May, Louise Pickford, James Porter, Annie Rigg,
Jenny Tschiesche, Laura Washburn Hutton and
Ryland Peters & Small 2025.
Design and photography © Ryland Peters & Small
2025. (See page 128 for full credits.)

ISBN: 978-1-78879-673-6

10 9 8 7 6 5 4 3 2 1

The authors' moral rights have been asserted.
All rights reserved. No part of this publication
may be reproduced, stored in a retrieval system
or transmitted in any form or by any means,
electronic, mechanical, photocopying or otherwise,
without the prior permission of the publisher.

A CIP record for this book is available from the
British Library.
US Library of Congress Cataloging-in-Publication
data has been applied for.

Printed and bound in China.

NOTES

• Both British (Metric) and American (Imperial
ounces plus US cups) are included in these
recipes for your convenience; however, it is
important to work with one set of
measurements only and not alternate between
the two within a recipe.

• All spoon measurements are level unless
otherwise specified.

• All eggs are medium (UK) or large (US), unless
specified as large, in which case US extra-large
should be used. Uncooked or partially cooked
eggs should not be served to the very old, frail,
young children, pregnant women or those with
compromised immune systems.

• Ovens should be preheated to the specified
temperatures. We recommend using an oven
thermometer. If using a fan-assisted oven,
adjust temperatures according to the
manufacturer's instructions.

• When a recipe calls for the grated zest of citrus
fruit, buy unwaxed fruit and wash well before
using. If you can only find treated fruit, scrub
well in warm soapy water before using.

• Many of the recipes include cooking with
hot oil, so care must be taken. See page 8 for
safety tips.

CONTENTS

INTRODUCTION

A simple sliver of potato immersed in bubbling oil — what's not to like? Very little, as the universal popularity of French fries demonstrates. People have their own preferences, for thick-cut or thinly sliced fries, with or without the potato skin, and then there's the array of dips and sauces to choose from. Everyone has their own special combination.

But who made the first French fry? They are thought to herald from either France or Belgium. The French story tells us that they were first sold by street vendors on the Pont Neuf in Paris, around the time of the 1789 Revolution. Belgians contest this, with one story claiming that potatoes were deep-fried before 1680 in the Meuse valley.

In any case, it is only in America that deep-fried potato slices have a French connection. In Belgium, they're called 'fries' or 'friet' (there's even a Frietmuseum in Bruges, which describes itself as 'the first and only museum dedicated to fries'), while in the Netherlands, they're called 'patat' and in France, 'les frites'. In the UK, they are called 'chips', and are doused with malt vinegar and served alongside battered fried fish and mushy peas.

What is beyond doubt is that everyone enjoys a French fry. Eat them with your fingers, a small wooden fork, or with fine cutlery and enjoy them simply salted, drowned in Dutch fashion with satay sauce, mayo and onions, or beneath a Korean-style beef and kimchi topping.

And while potatoes are the obvious choice for the deep fry, they are not the only ingredient that can be sliced and plunged into hot oil. Most root vegetables take kindly to this preparation, and this book includes recipes for more than just potato-based fries. More delicate vegetables, like celeriac and asparagus, get treated to a light crumb coating as well, and for the health-conscious, there is the occasional oven-baked recipe too. Something for everyone!

EQUIPMENT & TECHNIQUES

Frying can be performed with a few simple pieces of equipment:

DEEP FRYER

If you use a deep fryer, simply follow the manufacturer's instructions for filling it with oil and heating to temperature.

ON THE STOVETOP

You don't need a deep-fryer – the same results can be achieved with a few ordinary kitchen utensils and a heavy-bottomed saucepan with a depth of at least 10 cm/ 4 inches. It should be wide enough to allow a small batch of fries to be submerged.

COOKING THERMOMETER

A basic cooking thermometer that can be held upright in the middle of the pan will suffice. If you don't have one, test the oil temperature by adding a small cube of bread to the pan; it will turn golden in 10 seconds when the oil reaches 190°C (375°F), the ideal temperature for most of these recipes.

SLOTTED SPOON OR FRYING BASKET

To remove the fries, use an implement that lifts them out of the oil and allows them to drain over the pan for a few seconds. The handle should be long enough to keep your arm well away from spatters.

Whichever frying method you choose, the following techniques all apply:

TYPES OF OIL

Sunflower, peanut, soybean and vegetable oil are all neutral in flavour and have a high smoke point (the temperature at which the oil starts to break down and emit smoke), which makes them all good for frying.

ENSURE THAT THE FOOD IS DRY

Moisture on the food will cause the oil to spatter, so be sure to dry ingredients well before adding to the oil. The exception is for certain recipes that call for a light coating of cornflour/cornstarch paste.

DRAINING

Be sure to allow the food to drain on paper towels to absorb excess surface oil.

SAFETY TIPS

Deep-frying requires supervision and care and so be sure to keep an eye on the temperature of the oil. In the event of a grease fire, do not attempt to carry the pot; use a fire blanket, a damp towel or a fire extinguisher designed specifically for grease fires to suffocate the flames. Be sure to turn off the heat source as well. Never throw water on a grease fire as it will simply add fuel to the fire.

1
CLASSICS

CLASSIC FRIES

The simplicity of hot, crispy potatoes requires nothing more than some sea salt flakes as seasoning. If you do want a bit of a flourish, malt vinegar, mayonnaise or ketchup will do the trick.

3–4 large floury potatoes, all roughly the same size

vegetable or sunflower oil, for frying

sea salt flakes

SERVES 4

Peel the potatoes and trim on all sides to get a block. Cut the block into slices about 1-cm/½-inch thick, then cut the slices again to get fries/chips.

Put the potatoes into a bowl of iced water for 5 minutes, to remove excess starch and prevent sticking when frying.

Fill a large saucepan one-third full with oil or, if using a deep-fat fryer, follow the manufacturer's instructions. Heat the oil to 190°C/375°F or until a cube of bread browns in 30 seconds.

Drain the potatoes and dry very well. Working in batches, fry about a handful of potatoes at a time. Place the potatoes in a frying basket (or use a slotted metal spoon) and lower into the hot oil carefully. Fry for 4 minutes. Remove and drain on paper towels. Repeat until all of the potatoes have been fried.

Just before serving, skim any debris off the top of the cooking oil and reheat to the same temperature.

Fry as before, working in batches, but only cook for about 2 minutes until crisp and golden. Remove and drain on paper towels. Repeat until all of the potatoes have been fried.

Sprinkle with the salt flakes and serve.

MATCHSTICK FRIES WITH SICHUAN PEPPER SALT

Super-skinny, well seasoned and crunchy, matchstick fries make a great bar snack – enjoy these with a glass of chilled beer.

2 large floury potatoes, roughly the same size

cornflour/cornstarch, for coating

vegetable or sunflower oil, for deep frying

SICHUAN PEPPER SALT

1 tbsp Sichuan peppercorns

2 tbsp coarse rock salt

SERVES 4

For the Sichuan Pepper Salt, heat the peppercorns in a small frying pan/skillet until hot but not smoking. Transfer to a plate to cool. Combine with the salt, then grind in a spice mill or with a pestle and mortar. Set aside.

Peel the potatoes and trim on all sides to get a block. Cut the block into thin slices, then cut the slices thinly into matchsticks. Put the sticks into a bowl of iced water for at least 5 minutes. Put the cornflour in a shallow bowl.

Fill a saucepan one-third full with oil or, if using a deep-fat fryer, follow the manufacturer's instructions. Heat the oil to 190°C/375°F or until a cube of bread browns in 30 seconds.

Drain the potatoes and dry very well, then toss to coat lightly with the cornflour. Put in a sieve/strainer to help shake off any excess cornflour.

Working in batches, fry a handful of potatoes at a time. Place them in a frying basket and lower into the hot oil carefully. Fry for about 5 minutes. Remove and drain on paper towels. Repeat until all of the potatoes have been fried. Sprinkle with the Sichuan Pepper Salt and serve.

GARLIC & HERB POTATO WEDGES
WITH GARLIC LEMON MAYO

800 g/1¾ lb. floury potatoes, preferably Cyprus, scrubbed

4–5 tbsp vegetable oil

1 tsp fine salt

2 garlic cloves, crushed

1 tsp dried rosemary

1 tsp dried thyme

salt and black pepper

GARLIC LEMON MAYO

125 g/½ cup mayonnaise

2 garlic cloves, crushed

freshly squeezed juice of ½ lemon

SERVES 4–6

The smell of roasting garlic and rosemary infuses these potato wedges with sunny Mediterranean vibes. To keep the good feelings going, serve with a garlic lemon mayo dip and it will seem like summer, no matter what the weather.

Preheat the oven to 200°C/180°C fan/400°F/Gas 6. Line a large baking sheet with parchment paper.

In a small bowl, combine the mayonnaise, garlic and lemon juice and stir to mix. Set aside.

Cut the potatoes in half lengthwise, then into thirds so you end up with six long wedges. Put the wedges in a large mixing bowl and add the oil, salt, garlic, herbs and a generous grinding of pepper. Toss well with your hands to coat evenly, then transfer to the prepared sheets and spread evenly in a single layer.

Roast for 20 minutes in the preheated oven, then turn the potatoes and continue roasting for another 10–15 minutes until deep golden and cooked through. Sprinkle with salt and more pepper and serve with the garlic lemon mayo.

PAPRIKA & CHILLI FRIES

Although it might seem to some that fries or wedges should be prepared in a deep-fat fryer, cooking them in the oven actually delivers a better texture and crunch. It's also much easier to season them properly. These fries are crispy, golden and the perfect accompaniment to any sandwich or snack.

4 large baking potatoes

50 g/¼ cup olive oil

1 tbsp paprika

1 tbsp garlic powder

1 tbsp chilli/chili powder

1 tbsp onion powder

SERVES 4

Preheat an oven to 180°C/160°C fan/350°F/Gas 4.

Use a sharp knife to cut the potatoes into 2.5-cm/1-inch thick wedges. In a medium-size mixing bowl, mix together the olive oil, paprika, garlic powder, chilli powder and onion powder. Coat the potatoes in this oil and spice mixture and place them on a baking sheet.

Bake the fries for 45–60 minutes in the preheated oven, turning once, and remove when they're golden and crispy.

TRUFFLE FRIES

These are high-class so serve them with something of equal standing, like fillet steak. To get the best taste, use a very good brand of truffle oil.

2 kg/4½ lb. floury potatoes, all roughly the same size, peeled

vegetable or sunflower oil, for frying

1–2 tbsp high-quality truffle oil

sea salt flakes

SERVES 4

Peel the potatoes and trim on all sides to get a block. Cut the block into slices about 1-cm/½-inch thick, then cut the slices again to get fries/chips. Put the cut potatoes into a bowl of ice-cold water for at least 5 minutes.

Fill a large saucepan one-third full with oil or, if using a deep-fat fryer, follow the manufacturer's instructions. Heat the oil to 190°C/375°F or until a cube of bread browns in 30 seconds.

Drain the potatoes and dry very well. Working in batches, fry about a handful of potatoes at a time. Place the potatoes in a frying basket and lower into the hot oil carefully. Fry for about 3–4 minutes. Remove and drain on paper towels. Repeat until all of the potatoes have been fried.

Just before serving, skim any debris off the top of the cooking oil and reheat to the same temperature. Fry as before, working in batches, but only cook for about 2 minutes until crisp and golden. Remove and drain on paper towels. Repeat until all of the potatoes have been fried.

Toss with 1 tablespoon of the truffle oil, sprinkle with the salt flakes and taste. Add more oil if desired, then serve while still piping hot.

RUSTIC STEAK FRIES

Something about the size of these skin-on fries means they marry well with powerful flavours, so it's a good idea to use strong spices or dips.

3 large floury potatoes, all roughly the same size

vegetable or sunflower oil, for frying

SEASONED SALT

2 tbsp fine salt

1 tsp caster/granulated sugar

½ tsp celery salt

½ tsp paprika

¼ tsp ground turmeric

¼ tsp onion granules

¼ tsp garlic granules

pinch of cayenne pepper

SERVES 4

In a small bowl, combine the seasoning ingredients and mix well to blend. Set aside.

Scrub the potatoes well and dry. Cut the potatoes into long thin pieces, not as big as a wedge but not as small as a fry. Do not peel.

Put the potatoes into a bowl of iced water for at least 5 minutes, to remove excess starch and prevent sticking when frying.

Fill a large saucepan one-third full with the oil or, if using a deep-fat fryer, follow the manufacturer's instructions. Heat the oil to 190°C/375°F or until a cube of bread browns in about 30 seconds.

Drain the potatoes and dry very well. Working in batches, fry about a handful of potatoes at a time. Place the potatoes in a frying basket and lower into the hot oil carefully. Fry for about 4 minutes. Remove and drain on paper towels. Repeat until all of the potatoes have been fried.

Just before serving, skim any debris off the top of the cooking oil and reheat to the same temperature. Fry as before, working in batches, but only cook for about 2 minutes until crisp and golden. Remove and drain on paper towels.

Repeat until all of the potatoes have been fried. Serve with the seasoned salt on the side.

PIQUANT POTATO STRAWS

There is something completely irresistible about these dainty, crisp-textured potato straws. Serve them as an accompaniment for gin and tonics for pre-dinner drinks.

400 g/14 oz. potatoes

1 tsp hot smoked paprika or pimentón

1 tsp mild smoked paprika or pimentón

1–2 tsp salt

oil, for deep-frying

SERVES 8–10 AS A NIBBLE

Peel the potatoes and cut into short, extra-thin matchstick strips. Rinse in cold water, then pat dry thoroughly.

Heat enough oil for deep-frying in a deep pan or wok to 180°C/350°F or until a small piece of bread added to the hot oil browns within 60 seconds.

Fry the potato straws in batches, so as not to overcrowd the pan. Cook them until they turn golden brown on all sides, remove with a slotted spoon and drain on paper towels.

Toss the freshly fried potato straws at once with the two types of paprika or pimentón and the salt, mixing thoroughly. Serve at once.

TRIPLE-COOKED FRIES

This triple-cooking method produces golden brown fries, which are crisp on the outside and tender inside – a tempting combination.

800 g/1¾ lb. large floury potatoes, roughly the same size

vegetable or sunflower oil, for frying

salt

mayonnaise, to serve

SERVES 4

Peel the potatoes and trim on all sides to get a block. Cut the block into slices about 1-cm/½-inch thick, then cut the slices again to get fries/chips. Put the cut potatoes into a bowl of ice-cold water for at least 5 minutes.

Place the fries in a pan, cover with cold, salted water. Bring to the boil, then reduce the heat and simmer for 5 minutes; drain. Cover the par-boiled fries with cold water to cool, drain and chill in the fridge for 30 minutes to firm up.

Heat enough oil for deep-frying in a deep-fat fryer or a deep pan to a temperature of 130°C/250°F. Add in the chilled fries, cooking in batches so as not to overcrowd the pan, and fry each batch for 5 minutes. They should remain pale and not take on any colour. Remove with a slotted spoon, drain on paper towels and leave to cool.

Heat the same oil for deep-frying in the deep-fat fryer or a deep pan to a temperature of 180°C/350°F. Add the cooled fries, frying them in batches so as not to overcrowd the pan, for 3–5 minutes until golden brown and crisp. Remove with a slotted spoon, drain on paper towels, season with salt and serve at once with mayonnaise on the side.

SWEET POTATO FRIES

Although not the traditional potato fry, the classics chapter wouldn't be complete without the fantastic sweet potato version. The natural sweetness of the sweet potato and the caramelization when cooked really elevates the fry to a whole new level.

3 large sweet potatoes, unpeeled and chopped into chunky fries

1 tsp sea salt

1 bulb of garlic, cloves separated, skin left on and lightly crushed

½ bunch of fresh thyme, sprigs snapped in half

olive oil, for drizzling

dips of your choice, to serve

SERVES 4–8

Preheat the oven to 245°C/220°C fan/475°F/Gas 9.

Add the potatoes to a large saucepan. Cover them entirely with water and add the salt – this helps to remove the starch. Bring to the boil and cook over a high heat for 5–10 minutes. You will know the potatoes are done when the water starts to foam (or the water begins a rolling boil). The fries should be soft but still firm to the touch.

Remove from the heat and drain the fries, washing them in cold water using a sieve. This stops the fries overcooking.

Transfer the fries to a roasting tin and add the garlic and thyme. Drizzle with olive oil until the fries are well coated, then add 50 ml/3½ tablespoons water.

Cover the roasting tin with foil, then roast in the preheated oven for 30–40 minutes until the fries are soft and slightly charred. If the potatoes are not charred after 30 minutes, remove the foil, return them to the oven and let them crisp. Serve hot and enjoy with your favourite dipping sauces.

PATATAS BRAVAS WEDGES

A classic alternative to the standard potato chip/fry, these Mediterranean potato bites will add a sunny taste to any meal.

2 large potatoes

2 orange-fleshed sweet potatoes

4 tbsp olive oil

1 onion, chopped

2 garlic cloves, sliced

1 tsp coriander seeds

1 tsp cumin seeds

1 tsp Spanish smoked paprika

big pinch of crushed dried chillies

150 g/5 oz. cherry tomatoes

salt and black pepper

freshly chopped flat-leaf parsley, to garnish

SERVES 4

Preheat the oven to 225°C/200°C fan/425°F/Gas 7.

Peel and cut the large potatoes into large, bite-size wedges or chunks, tip into a saucepan of salted water and bring to the boil. Cook over a medium heat for about 5–7 minutes. Drain and leave the potatoes to dry in the colander.

Peel and cut the sweet potato into chunks the same size as the other potatoes and tip into a roasting dish. Add the blanched potatoes, drizzle half the olive oil over them and roast in the preheated oven for about 30 minutes, or until lightly golden and tender.

Meanwhile, heat the remaining olive oil in a frying pan/ skillet. Add the onion and cook for about 2–3 minutes until tender but not coloured. Add the garlic and spices and cook for another 2 minutes until golden and fragrant. Add the cherry tomatoes to the pan and continue to cook until they start to soften.

Tip the contents of the pan into the roasting dish with the potatoes, season with salt and black pepper, stir to combine and return to the oven for another 5 minutes.

Serve warm, garnished with the chopped parsley.

2
VEG FRIES

OVEN-BAKED BEETROOT FRIES
WITH WASABI MAYO

Opposites attract, which is why sweet, roasted beet(root) goes so well with a spicy Japanese wasabi mayo and a sesame-chilli seasoned salt.

2 kg/4½ lb. beet(root)

2–3 tbsp vegetable oil

fine salt

2–3 tsp Togarashi (Japanese seven spice) seasoning or black sesame seeds and chilli/ hot red pepper flakes

WASABI MAYO

125 g/½ cup mayonnaise

1 spring onion/scallion, finely sliced

¼ tsp wasabi paste, or to taste

SERVES 4

In a small bowl, combine the mayonnaise ingredients and mix well to blend. Set aside.

Preheat the oven to 200°C/180°C fan/400°F/Gas 6. Line a large baking sheet with parchment paper.

Scrub the beetroot and trim the ends. Cut into 1-cm/½-inch thick slices, and then again into 1-cm/½-inch batons.

Transfer to the prepared baking sheet and spread evenly in a single layer. Drizzle over the oil and season lightly with salt. Bake in the preheated oven for about 25–35 minutes until tender and starting to crisp.

Remove from the oven and transfer to a serving dish. Sprinkle with the Togarashi seasoning (or black sesame seeds and chilli flakes) and serve with the mayonnaise.

OVEN-BAKED CELERIAC FRIES
WITH HONEY & THYME

This is a sophisticated and carb-free French-fry alternative. The honey complements the distinctive taste of this subtle root vegetable and also helps to give it a deep caramel colour as it bakes.

30 g/2 tbsp unsalted butter

1 tbsp clear honey

1–2 tbsp vegetable oil

1 large celeriac

1 small bunch of fresh thyme

salt and black pepper

SERVES 2—4

Preheat the oven to 200°C/180°C fan/400°F/Gas 6. Line a large baking sheet with parchment paper.

Combine the butter and honey in a small saucepan and melt over a low heat. Alternatively, melt in the microwave. Stir in 1 tablespoon of the oil and set aside.

Remove the skin from the celeriac with a small knife, or use a vegetable peeler. Cut the celeriac into 1-cm/½-inch thick slices, and then again into 1-cm/½-inch batons.

Immediately put the celeriac fries into a large bowl, add the butter mixture and toss well to coat. Add a bit more oil if there is not enough. Season with salt, then transfer to the prepared baking sheet and spread evenly in a single layer. Scatter over the thyme sprigs and bake in the preheated oven for about 25–35 minutes until browned.

Remove from the oven, season lightly with salt and pepper and serve at once.

CUMIN CARROT FRIES

Sweet and spicy, carrots and cumin combine so well and are perfectly crisp when cooked in an air fryer. Serve as a snack or as a side dish.

300 g/10½ oz. carrots

1 tsp cornflour/cornstarch

1 tsp ground cumin

¼ tsp salt

1 tbsp olive oil

Aioli (see page 115), for dipping

an air-fryer

SERVES 2

Preheat the air-fryer to 200°C/400°F.

Peel the carrots and cut into thin fries, roughly 10 x 1 cm x 5 mm/4 x ½ x ¼ inches. Toss the carrots in a bowl with all the other ingredients.

Add the carrots to the preheated air-fryer and air-fry for 9 minutes, shaking the drawer of the air-fryer a couple of times during cooking. Serve with garlic mayo on the side.

HERBY SWEDE FRIES

Ideal for those who love the idea of fries but want a lower carb and lower fat alternative as these are baked in an air fryer.

1 medium swede/
rutabaga

½ tsp salt

½ tsp freshly ground
black pepper

1½ tsp dried thyme

1 tbsp olive oil

an air-fryer

SERVES 4

Preheat the air-fryer to 160°C/325°F.

Peel the swede and slice into fries about 6 x 1 cm/2½ x ½ inches, then toss the fries in the salt, pepper, thyme and oil, making sure every fry is coated.

Tip into the preheated air-fryer in a single layer (you may need to cook them in two batches, depending on the size of your air-fryer) and air-fry for 15 minutes, shaking the drawer halfway through.

Increase the temperature to 180°C/350°F and cook for a further 5 minutes. Serve immediately.

AUBERGINE & SUMAC FRIES

500 g/1 lb. 2 oz. aubergine/eggplant, ends trimmed and cut into 2-cm/¾-inch wide strips

125 g/1 cup rice flour

1 tbsp sumac, plus extra to serve

2–3 sprigs fresh mint, leaves stripped and very finely chopped

1 tsp fine salt

vegetable oil

1 tbsp toasted sesame seeds

TO SERVE

lemon wedges

a few sprigs fresh mint

Lemon & Tahini Dip (see page 120)

SERVES 2—4

The velvety smooth texture of aubergine/eggplant is the perfect vehicle for some wonderful Middle Eastern ingredients. Zingy, zesty and fresh, serve this at lunch with a selection of salads or with scrambled eggs for a new twist on brunch.

A few hours before serving (ideally 2–12 hours), put the aubergine in a large bowl and add cold water and some ice to cover. Set a plate on top to weigh the aubergine down; it must stay submerged.

When ready to cook, combine the rice flour, sumac, chopped mint and salt in a shallow bowl and mix well.

Fill a large saucepan one-third full with the oil or, if using a deep-fat fryer, follow the manufacturer's instructions. Heat the oil to 190°C/375°F or until a cube of bread browns in 30 seconds.

Working in batches, transfer the damp aubergine to the rice flour mixture and coat lightly. Place in a frying basket and lower into the hot oil carefully. Fry for 3–4 minutes until golden. Remove and drain on paper towels. Repeat until all of the aubergine has been fried.

Mound on a platter and scatter over the sesame seeds, some sumac and the mint leaves. Serve with lemon wedges and the dipping sauce.

CRISPY COURGETTE FRIES

Courgettes/zucchini are not always a popular vegetable. However, try coating them in this seasoned cheesy crumb to turn them into something irresistible.

1 courgette/zucchini

3 tbsp plain/all-purpose flour

¼ tsp salt

¼ tsp black pepper

60 g/¾ cup dried breadcrumbs

1 tsp dried oregano

20 g/¼ cup finely grated Parmesan

1 egg, beaten

an air-fryer

SERVES 2

Preheat the air-fryer to 180°C/350°F.

Slice the courgette into fries about 1.5-cm/¾-inch thick.

Season the flour with salt and pepper. Combine the dried breadcrumbs with the oregano and Parmesan.

Dip the courgettes in the flour (shaking off any excess flour), then the egg, then the seasoned breadcrumbs.

Add the fries to the preheated air-fryer and air-fry for about 15 minutes. They should be crispy on the outside but soft on the inside. Serve immediately.

LEMON-PEPPER ASPARAGUS FRIES

As asparagus is practically shaped like a French fry to start with, they lend themselves well to a dunk in beaten egg and a covering of crispy crumb for a satisfying and guilt-free fry.

200 g/4 cups panko breadcrumbs

1 tbsp coarse-ground black pepper

½ tsp fine salt

50 g/3 tbsp self-raising/ rising flour

zest of 1 lemon

2 eggs

500 g/1 lb. 2 oz. asparagus spears, trimmed

lemon wedges and your choice of dip, to serve

SERVES 2—4

Preheat the oven to 200°C/180°C fan/400°F/Gas 6. Line a baking sheet with parchment paper.

Combine the panko breadcrumbs, black pepper, salt, flour and lemon zest in a shallow dish long enough to fit the length of the asparagus; a baking dish works well.

Put the eggs in a shallow bowl and beat well.

Working one at a time, dip the asparagus spears into the egg wash and let the excess drip off, then coat in the panko mixture. Arrange the spears in a single layer on the prepared baking sheet as you go. It helps if you use one hand for the egg dip and the other for the breadcrumbs.

Bake for about 15–20 minutes until browned and crisp.

Serve hot, with the lemon wedges and your choice of dip.

Tip: these crispy fries work especially well with a lemony mayonnaise dip.

BAKED AUBERGINE FRIES WITH BBQ DIP

These vegan baked aubergine/eggplant fries can be served simply drizzled with a little balsamic vinegar or with this tangy vegan BBQ dip.

1 medium–large aubergine/eggplant

2–3 tbsp potato flour or cornflour/cornstarch

4 tbsp aquafaba (chickpea liquid)

80 g/2 cups panko breadcrumbs

20 g/½ cup nutritional yeast

1 tsp rock salt

vegetable oil spray

VEGAN BBQ DIP

500 ml/2 cups ketchup

60 ml/¼ cup cider vinegar

60 ml/¼ cup vegan Worcester sauce

50 g/¼ cup unrefined brown sugar

2 tbsp molasses

2 tbsp yellow mustard

1 tbsp hot sauce

1 tbsp BBQ seasoning

½ tsp ground black pepper

baking sheet, lightly oiled

SERVES 2–3

Preheat the oven to 220°C/200°C fan/425°F/Gas 7. Lightly spray or grease a baking sheet with oil.

Slice the aubergine at an angle, into 2.5 cm/1 inch thick discs, then slice each disc into 2.5 cm/ 1 inch thick batons. Place the potato flour on a small plate. Place the aquafaba in one bowl and in a larger bowl, mix the breadcrumbs, nutritional yeast and salt.

Dip the aubergine fries into the potato flour, then into the aquafaba and toss them in the breadcrumbs.

Lay the coated batons onto the lightly oiled baking sheet. Spray lightly with a little vegetable oil. Bake in the preheated oven for 20–25 minutes, turning once or

twice to ensure they are golden and crispy all over.

While they are baking, add all the BBQ sauce ingredients to a small pan and place over medium-high heat. Bring to a simmer, and stir well until the sauce is thick and glossy. Set aside to cool. This sauce will keep for several weeks in the fridge if stored in a sterilized container.

Serve the aubergine fries hot from the oven, with the BBQ sauce for dipping.

Tip: these are also delicious served with a dip of soya yogurt mixed with garlic and herbs.

PLANTAIN WEDGES WITH MANGO SALSA

vegetable oil, for frying

3–4 ripe plantain, peeled and chopped into 2.5-cm/1-inch chunks

jerk salt or seasoning, for dusting (optional)

SALSA

½ mango, stoned/pitted, peeled and diced

½ red onion, diced

¼ Scotch bonnet pepper, finely diced

¼ bunch of fresh chives, snipped

2 fresh thyme sprigs, leaves removed

grated zest and juice of ½ lime

SERVES 2–4

Plantain is a staple in African and Caribbean cooking. It is highly versatile and makes the perfect fried side. Nothing beats just simple good old fried plantain.

First, make the salsa. Place all the ingredients in a bowl and mix everything together. Set aside for later.

Heat a shallow heavy-based saucepan with oil about 2 cm/ ¾ inch deep. Fry the plantain for 2 minutes for really ripe plantain and 4 minutes for less ripe plantain until golden all over. Be careful not to overcook them, as the plantain will continue to cook from the residual heat once removed from the pan. Remove from the pan with a slotted spoon and drain any excess oil on a plate lined with paper towels.

Serve the plantain wedges hot with the mango salsa and with an added dusting of jerk salt or seasoning if liked.

Tips
• The ripe plantain should be yellow in colour with some black markings. Plantain that are too black are overripe.
• These wedges can also be deep-fried. Heat the oil to about 180°C/350°F on a thermometer. Otherwise, to check the oil is hot enough, flick a little water into the oil; if the oil spits back at you, it is hot enough to continue. When the wedges are golden, they are ready to serve.

3
OTHER FRIED SIDES

LEMON & PECORINO POLENTA FRIES

These fries are just so good. Try loading the polenta/cornmeal with lots of different flavours – it's great with herbs, spices, cheeses and the like.

400 ml/1¾ cups vegetable stock

100 ml/⅓ cup full-fat/ whole milk

150 g/1 cup polenta/ cornmeal, plus extra for coating

50 g/2 oz. Pecorino, finely grated/ shredded

1 lemon, zested, then cut into wedges

olive oil, for baking

salt and pepper

large baking sheet lined with parchment paper

SERVES 4

Put the vegetable stock and milk (with a good grind of pepper) in a medium saucepan and bring to just below the boil. When the liquid has come to temperature, add the polenta and stir continuously, until all the liquid has been absorbed. Continue stirring constantly until the mix is thick and coming away from the side of the pan. It should only take a minute or two. Remove from the heat and immediately add the Pecorino and lemon zest. Stir well to combine, then pile onto the lined baking sheet and spread out so it's smooth and about 1 cm/½ inch thick. Leave the polenta to cool for about 15 minutes.

Preheat the oven to 240°C/220°C fan/450°F/Gas 8.

Once cool, lift the polenta up using the baking paper and place on a chopping board. Slice the block up into 1-cm/½-inch thick, long fries as this makes for super crispy 'French fries'.

Using the same baking sheet (now without the paper), sprinkle a little dry polenta over the sheet, then spread out the fries on top. Sprinkle a little more dry polenta on top, and finish with a squeeze of lemon juice, a scant sprinkle of sea salt and a drizzle of olive oil. Place on the top shelf of the preheated oven and bake for 30 minutes, until very crispy.

Serve with the spare lemon wedges alongside for squeezing and a little extra grated Pecorino on top.

2 ripe but firm avocados, peeled, stoned/pitted and sliced

200 g/4 cups gluten-free breadcrumbs

50 g/3 tbsp self-raising/rising flour

½ tsp fine salt

½ tsp paprika

2 eggs

lime wedges, to serve

SOUR CREAM & CHIPOTLE DIP

150 ml/½ cup plus 1 tbsp sour cream

½ tsp chipotle paste

few sprigs fresh coriander/cilantro, finely chopped

zest and freshly squeezed juice of 1 lime

SERVES 2—4

AVOCADO FRIES WITH SOUR CREAM & CHIPOTLE DIP

Gluten-free breadcrumbs have a very fine texture and make a fantastic coating, perfect for encasing velvety rich wedges of avocado.

Preheat the oven to 200°C/180°C fan/400°F/Gas 6. Line a baking sheet with parchment paper.

Combine the breadcrumbs, flour, salt and paprika in a shallow dish.

Put the eggs in a shallow bowl and beat well.

Working one at a time, dip the avocado slices into the egg wash and let the excess drip off, then coat in the breadcrumb mixture. Arrange in a single layer on the prepared baking sheet as you go. It helps if you use one hand for the egg dip and the other for the breadcrumbs.

Bake in the preheated oven for about 15 minutes until browned and crisp.

Meanwhile, combine the Sour Cream & Chipotle Dip ingredients in a small bowl and stir well. Set aside.

Serve hot, with lime wedges and the dip.

HALLOUMI & ZA'ATAR FRIES

If ever there was a cheese that improves with cooking, it's halloumi, so it works fantastically well with crispy fries. Enjoy these salty, squeaky sticks with a rich beet(root) dip, or roll it all up in flatbread with some crisp lettuce, tomatoes and cucumber.

400 g/14 oz. halloumi

150 g/1 cup plain/ all-purpose flour

1 tbsp za'atar, plus extra to serve

vegetable oil

lemon wedges, to serve

Beetroot, Yogurt & Mint Dip (see page 120)

SERVES 2—4

Cut the halloumi into 2-cm/¾-inch wide strips.

Mix the flour and za'atar together in a shallow bowl.

Fill a large saucepan one-third full with the oil or, if using a deep-fat fryer, follow the manufacturer's instructions. Heat the oil to 190°C/375°F or until a cube of bread browns in 30 seconds.

Working in batches, coat the halloumi strips in the flour mixture. Place in a frying basket and lower into the hot oil carefully. Fry for 3—4 minutes until golden. Remove and drain on paper towels. Repeat until all of the halloumi has been fried.

To serve, mound on a platter and scatter over some za'atar. Serve with lemon wedges and the dipping sauce.

SWEETCORN-SAGE POLENTA FRIES

These golden polenta fries, flecked with sweet nuggets of corn kernels, go really well with grilled or fried chicken.

1 tbsp fine salt

250 g/1½ cups plus 2 tbsp quick-cook polenta/cornmeal

100 g/¾ cup sweetcorn/corn kernels

2 tsp dried sage leaves, crumbled

3 tbsp grated/shredded Parmesan, plus extra to serve

plain/all-purpose flour, for dusting

vegetable oil, for frying

black pepper

Chilli Ketchup (see page 113), to serve

SERVES 4

Lightly grease a large baking sheet, about 1.5-cm/⅝-inch deep, with vegetable oil.

In a large saucepan, bring 1.5 litres/quarts water to the boil. Add the salt and stir to dissolve. Lower the heat to very low and begin stirring gently with a wooden spoon. As you stir, pour in the polenta in a steady stream. Continue stirring and add the sweetcorn and sage. Cook for 3 minutes, stirring constantly.

Pour the polenta into the prepared baking sheet and spread out evenly, to the thickness of a French fry. Let cool for 20 minutes, then refrigerate for 1 hour to cool completely.

Invert the chilled polenta onto a clean work surface and cut into 8-cm/3-inch long sticks. Put the flour in a dish.

Fill a large saucepan one-third full with the oil or, if using a deep-fat fryer, follow manufacturer's instructions. Heat the oil to 190°C/375°F or until a cube of bread browns in 30 seconds.

Working in batches, lightly coat the polenta sticks in flour. Place in a frying basket and lower into the hot oil carefully. Fry for about 3–4 minutes until golden. Remove and drain on paper towels. Repeat until all of the sticks have been fried.

To serve, mound on a platter and sprinkle with Parmesan and black pepper and the dipping sauce.

PARMESAN PARSNIP FRIES

The best alternative to potato fries and a great way to disguise vegetables for a kids meal.

500 g/1 lb. 2 oz. parsnips

100 g/¾ cup plain/all-purpose flour

2 eggs

50 ml/3 tbsp whole milk

200 g/1¼ cups polenta/cornmeal

50 g/¾ cup Parmesan, finely grated/shredded

vegetable oil, for frying

salt and black pepper

mayonnaise, to serve

SERVES 2—4

Scrub the parsnips well and pat dry thoroughly. Cut each parsnip in half crosswise to get two shorter pieces, then halve lengthwise. If the pieces are thick, cut into quarters lengthwise (the top halves will probably need to be quartered but not the bottoms).

Put the flour on a small plate. Combine the eggs and milk in a small bowl, whisk and set aside. Combine the polenta, Parmesan and a pinch of salt and pepper on a plate, mix well and set aside.

Bring a large pot of water to the boil, then add the parsnips and cook until just tender but not completely soft. Test by inserting the tip of a knife; you should still get some resistance. Time depends on size but about 5 minutes. Drain.

Coat the parsnips in the flour, then dip in the egg mixture and transfer immediately to the polenta mix and coat all over. Set aside and continue until all the pieces of parsnip are coated.

Fill a large saucepan one-third full with the oil or, if using a deep-fat fryer, follow the manufacturer's instructions. Heat the oil to 190°C/375°F or until a cube of bread browns in 30 seconds.

Working in batches, use tongs or a large wire-mesh skimmer to transfer the parsnips to the hot oil carefully. Fry for 3–5 minutes until golden. Remove and drain on paper towels. Repeat until all of the parsnips have been fried. Sprinkle with a bit more salt and serve with mayonnaise.

BEER-BATTERED AVOCADO WEDGES

6–8 ripe avocados

vegetable oil, for deep-frying

Roast Garlic & Chipotle Mayo (see page 15), to serve

FOR THE BATTER
165 g/1⅓ cups self-raising/rising flour

1 tsp salt

1 tsp cumin

1 tsp dried oregano

1½ tsp paprika

½ tsp black pepper

1 tsp ground avocado leaf powder (optional)

1 tsp baking powder

1 bottle (330 ml/11 fl oz.) lager of choice

SERVES 6–8

The combination of the crispy batter and the soft avocado centre is amazing in these unusual fries.

For the batter, mix together all the dry ingredients until they are well combined. Gently stir in the beer until you have a smooth batter and then put to one side.

Cut the avocados in half, peel them and remove the stones. Slice each half into 3–4 pieces lengthwise, depending on their size.

Pour enough oil into a medium saucepan to reach halfway up the side and heat until hot but not smoking.

Working with one avocado at a time, dip the slices in the batter until well covered, then carefully lower into the oil – it's best to use a slotted spoon to do this to avoid spitting oil.

Fry each batch for about 1 minute until the batter is golden, but no darker, and crispy. Remove the slices with a slotted spoon and place on a plate lined with paper towels to soak up any excess oil. Repeat with the remaining avocado slices.

Arrange the avocado slices on the plate, serve with the mayo and watch your friends' amazement when they try this dish!

DEEP-FRIED MOZZARELLA STICKS

Warm, crispy, gooey cheese sticks can't be beaten. Serve these mozzarella sticks with an array of the dips or sauces in this book.

2 eggs, beaten

120 g/1½ cups Italian-seasoned breadcrumbs

½ tsp garlic salt

80 g/⅔ cup plain/all-purpose flour

40 g/⅓ cup cornflour/cornstarch

450-g/1-lb. bag of mozzarella cheese sticks

vegetable oil, for frying

SERVES 4–6

In a small bowl, mix the eggs with 60 ml/¼ cup water.

In a separate bowl, mix the breadcrumbs and garlic salt.

In another bowl, mix the flour and cornflour.

Preheat the oil in a deep fryer set to 180°C/350°F.

One at a time, coat each mozzarella stick in flour, then egg and then breadcrumbs.

Fry for about 30 seconds until golden brown. Drain on paper towels before serving.

ALE-BATTERED ONION RINGS

Onion rings and French fries often compete for the title of main side dish. Although French fries are more common, it isn't until you have an onion ring in your mouth that you realize that if you were given the option, you would eat onion rings far more often.

120 g/1 cup plain/
all-purpose flour,
plus extra for dusting

250 ml/1 cup India pale
ale

2 large brown or Vidalia
onions

canola oil, for frying

salt

your choice of dips,
to serve

SERVES 4

Put the flour into a mixing bowl and make a well in the centre. Pour the ale into the well and whisk until combined. Let the mixture rest, covered for 1 hour.

Peel the onions and cut crosswise into 1-cm/½-inch thick rings. Dust the rings with more flour, shaking off the excess, and coat them with the batter.

Heat 5 cm/2 inches. of canola oil in a large frying pan/skillet. The pan is at the right temperature when the oil is steadily bubbling. Working in batches, fry the onion rings until they're golden in colour. Use a slotted spoon to transfer the onion rings onto paper towels to drain. Sprinkle them with salt to taste.

Dip them in ranch dressing and yellow mustard.

TATER TOTS

Tater tots are bite-size hash browns. Dip them in ketchup and serve them hot as a snack to make kids excited and adults nostalgic.

8 medium potatoes

1 tbsp plain/all-purpose flour

2 tbsp very finely chopped white onions

vegetable oil, for frying

salt and black pepper

SERVES 4

Cook the potatoes, unpeeled, in a pan of boiling water until tender. As soon as they are cool enough to handle, peel them and then finely grate/shred them or use a ricer. Stir in the flour, 1 teaspoon of salt, a pinch of black pepper and the chopped onion

Heat 5 mm/¼ inch of the oil for frying in a heavy-bottomed frying pan/skillet.

Form the potato mixture into small balls. Carefully drop the potato balls into the hot oil, in batches, and fry until slightly golden. Remove with a slotted spoon and drain on paper towels. Serve immediately.

BAKED POTATO SKINS WITH BUTTER

Make this genius snack when you have leftover potato skin halves, having made mashed potato with baked potato flesh (the best way to make particularly flavoursome mash). Eat them like a cracker or toast and you'll never look back.

baked potato skins, flesh removed

sea salt, butter and cheese, to serve

SERVES 2–4

Preheat the oven to 220°C/200°C fan/ 425°F/Gas 7.

Put the empty baked potato skins on a baking sheet and bake in the oven for 15–20 minutes to crisp up very well.

Let them sit for a minute before serving, then pop them on a board with butter, sea salt and cheese.

POTATO PEEL CHIPS

A great way to use up abandoned potato peelings.

peel from 1 kg/35 oz. of potatoes (I use red potatoes)

½ tsp smoked paprika

salt and black pepper

olive oil, for baking

SERVES 2–4

Preheat the oven to 200°C fan/220°C/425°F/Gas 7.

Chuck the peel on a non-stick baking sheet with a glug of olive oil, the smoked paprika and generous amounts of sea salt and black pepper. Toss well to coat and roast on the top shelf of the oven for 30 minutes; shake and turn a couple of times during the cooking time.

Cool on the sheet, tossing a couple of times, and either eat immediately as a cooking snack or transfer to a sealable container for snacking on later.

CORN 'RIBS'

Corn 'ribs' have become a bit of a social media sensation during the last few years, and make a great alternative to potato fries if you want to serve something different at a barbecue. These curly corn 'ribs' are topped with a delicious Indonesian-inspired sauce.

4 large corn cobs/ears, or use frozen and fully defrosted

½ tsp coriander seeds

½ tsp cumin seeds

½ tbsp extra-virgin coconut oil or vegetable oil

1 small brown onion, finely chopped

2 fat garlic cloves, finely chopped, or use 2 tsp garlic paste

2.5-cm/1-inch thumb of fresh ginger, peeled and finely chopped, or 1 heaped tbsp ginger paste

2–4 small red Thai chillies/chiles, finely chopped, to taste

1 tsp ground turmeric

1 tsp salt, or to taste

1 large tomato, roughly chopped, or use ½ x 400-g/14-oz. can tomatoes, drained

3–4 tbsp coconut cream, or use the thickest part of canned coconut milk

1 tsp date syrup, pure maple syrup or unrefined coconut sugar

1 lime

2 tbsp red-skinned peanuts, toasted and roughly chopped

handful of freshly chopped coriander/cilantro

1 tbsp desiccated/dried unsweetened shredded coconut, lightly toasted

baking sheet, lined with parchment

SERVES 4

Preheat the oven to 220°C/200°C fan/425°F/Gas 7.

Using a sharp knife, slice the corn cobs lengthwise into quarters.

Place a frying pan/skillet over medium heat and add the coriander and cumin seeds. Lightly toast for 1 minute, then add half the coconut oil. Add the chopped onion to the pan and fry gently for 2 minutes, then add the garlic, ginger, chillies, turmeric and salt. Mix well and cook for 2 minutes.

Add the tomato and 2 tablespoons water. Bring to a simmer and cook over low heat for 5 minutes until the tomato has completely broken down. Add the coconut cream and date syrup, mix well and check the seasoning, adding more salt if needed.

Rub the corn ribs with the remaining oil and arrange them on the lined baking sheet. Roast in the preheated oven for 15–20 minutes until golden brown.

Using a zester, remove the rind from the lime, roughly chop it (not too fine) and set aside. Halve the lime and add 1 tablespoon of the juice to the sauce.

Pile up the (now curvy) corn ribs onto a big platter and drizzle with the sauce. Sprinkle with the toasted peanuts, fresh coriander, coconut and lime rind. Serve immediately.

Tip: If you don't have corn cobs, you can simply add canned corn to the sauce and serve as a kind of corn curry.

BEER-BATTERED PICKLES

Give the quintessential dill pickle a new lease of life with this taste sensation. A perfect accompaniment to a burger or fried chicken meal.

4 large dill pickles

80 g/scant ⅔ cup potato flour

80 g/scant ⅔ cup plain/all-purpose flour

½ tbsp Korean red pepper powder

1 teaspoon fine salt

330-ml/12-oz. bottle of IPA or beer (substitute sparkling/soda water if you prefer)

400 ml/scant 1¾ cups sunflower oil, for frying

SERVES 4

Slice the dill pickles in half lengthwise. Mix together the flour, potato flour, red pepper powder and salt in a bowl. Add the beer and mix to form a runny batter that just coats the back of a spoon.

Heat the oil for deep-frying in a small, deep pan over medium-high heat. Check the oil is hot enough by dropping a little batter into the pan. If it sizzles and rises, the oil is ready.

Carefully dip the pickles into the batter and place into the hot oil. Fry in batches of 3–4, cooking for about 6–7 minutes until golden and crispy. Drain on paper towels.

BOCCONCINI BALLS

Bocconcini are small mozzarella balls. In this recipe they're breaded, then cooked in an air-fryer until melted on the inside and crisp and golden on the outside. Think mozzarella sticks but round! These are great served as a snack or with a salad as a light meal.

70 g/½ cup plain/all-purpose flour

1 egg, beaten

70 g/1 cup dried breadcrumbs

10 bocconcini

an air-fryer

SERVES 2

Preheat the air-fryer to 200°C/400°F.

Place the flour, egg and breadcrumbs on 3 separate plates. Dip each bocconcini ball first in the flour to coat, then the egg, shaking off any excess before rolling in the breadcrumbs.

Add the breaded bocconcini to the preheated air-fryer and air-fry for 5 minutes (no need to turn them during cooking). Serve immediately.

FRIED GREEN TOMATOES

This recipe is so simple to prepare – frying unripened tomatoes in vegetable oil after coating them with a mixture of flour, cornmeal and a little salt and pepper for extra seasoning.

4 large green tomatoes

2 eggs

125 ml/½ cup milk

120 g/1 cup plain/ all-purpose flour

65 g/½ cup cornmeal

60 g/½ cup panko or ordinary breadcrumbs

2 tsp coarse sea salt

¼ tsp black pepper

vegetable oil, for frying

SERVES 4

Chop the tomatoes into 1-cm/½-inch thick slices, discarding the ends. You should have 4–5 pieces per tomato. Set aside on a large plate.

In a medium bowl, whisk the eggs and milk together.

Measure out the flour and put it on a plate. In a separate bowl, whisk together the cornmeal, breadcrumbs, salt and pepper and transfer the mixture to a plate.

First, dip the tomato slices into the flour to coat, then dip them into the milk and egg mixture. Finally, dip them into the breadcrumb mixture so that they are completely covered in them.

Pour vegetable oil to a depth of 1 cm/½ inches into a large frying pan/skillet and heat over a medium heat. When the oil is steadily bubbling, carefully place the tomatoes into the frying pan in batches of 4 or 5, depending on the size of your frying pan. Do not crowd the tomatoes – they should not touch each other. When the tomatoes are browned, flip and fry them on the other side. Drain them on paper towels.

GREEN PLANTAIN FRITTERS

This can be a tricky recipe to prepare – as green plantain skin can be hard to remove – but they work perfectly as a refreshing, yet crispy element to any meal.

2–4 green plantain (see Note opposite), topped and tailed

2–3 tbsp garlic powder

1 tsp table salt

1 tbsp freshly ground black pepper

vegetable oil, for frying

SERVES 4–6

Carefully run a knife down the back of the plantain, scoring the skin, then peel off the skin – this can be quite tricky. If the skin is quite hard, cut the skin off as though peeling potatoes. Grate the plantain into a bowl, cover with water and leave to soak for at least 20 minutes – but up to 3 hours for the best results. This helps to remove the starch.

Drain the plantain through a sieve and pat dry to remove any excess liquid. Place the plantain in a mixing bowl and add the garlic powder, salt and pepper. Don't be afraid to be heavy-handed with the garlic powder.

Loosely roll the grated plantain into small 2.5-cm/1-inch sized balls. Be careful not to flatten the balls too much or roll them too tightly, or they will not cook in the centre.

Heat a shallow frying pan/skillet with oil about 4 cm/ 2½ inches deep. Fry the fritters for 10 minutes until they are golden brown and crispy all the way. Remove from the pan with a slotted spoon and drain any excess oil on a plate lined with paper towels. Serve with hot sauce for dipping, if liked.

Notes

• It is important to use the correct type of plantain as ripe plantain will not work – you need green plantain or 'green' banana.

• Please note that garlic granules or garlic salt will not work with this recipe. Garlic powder will give the best results as it dissolves easily.

• These fritters can also be deep-fried. Heat the oil to about 180°C/350°F on a thermometer. Otherwise, to check the oil is hot enough, flick a little water into the oil; if the oil spits back at you, it is hot enough to continue. When the wedges are golden, they are ready to serve.

MANCHEGO CHEESE BALLS

2 tbsp plain/all-purpose flour

2 tbsp milk

½ tsp oak-smoked sweet Spanish paprika

1 egg

1 garlic clove, crushed

150 g/6 oz. Manchego cheese, finely grated

150 g/6 oz. soft goats' cheese, preferably Spanish

2 egg whites

1 tsp chopped fresh thyme leaves

1 tbsp Serrano ham, finely chopped

salt and white pepper

oil, for frying

SERVES 4

Manchego cheese is popular all over Spain – it is to the Spanish what Parmesan is to the Italians. The mix of Manchego sheep's cheese and Spanish goats' cheese balance each other perfectly in this unctuous snack.

Put the flour and milk in a bowl and stir until smooth. Add the paprika, salt, pepper and the whole egg. Add the garlic and both cheeses and mix well.

Put the egg whites in a bowl and whisk until stiff. Fold one-third into the flour mixture and mix well, then gently fold in the remaining egg whites, taking care not to lose all of the air. Sprinkle with the thyme and Serrano ham.

Fill a saucepan or deep-fryer one-third full of oil or to the manufacturer's recommended level and heat to 195°C/380°F.

Using a teaspoon, run the spoon through the mixture, collecting an even amount of thyme and Serrano ham, and drop a heaped spoonful into the hot oil. Cook for 3 minutes or until the mixture is golden brown. Drain on paper towels and serve immediately.

4
FULLY LOADED

BLUE CHEESE & BACON FRIES

Classic Fries (see page 13)

2 slices bacon, fried, to serve

100 g/¾ cup blue cheese, crumbled

handful chopped chives, to serve

BLUE CHEESE BÉCHAMEL

2 slices pancetta or bacon, finely chopped

50 g/3 tbsp unsalted butter

60 g/4 tbsp plain/ all-purpose flour

550 ml/1 pint milk

½ tsp salt

150 g/1¼ cups blue cheese, crumbled

black pepper

SERVES 4

Blue cheese dressing with crispy bacon is a classic salad dressing. The transition to French-fry topping is seamless, and possibly even better.

Prepare and cook the fries following the instructions on page 13.

In a frying pan/skillet, cook the pancetta or bacon for the bechamel over a medium-high heat until crispy. Set aside. Cook the 2 whole slices of bacon until crispy and set aside on paper towels.

Meanwhile, prepare the béchamel sauce. Melt the butter in a saucepan. Stir in the flour and cook, stirring constantly, for 1 minute. Pour in the milk in a steady stream, whisking constantly and continue whisking gently for 3–5 minutes until the sauce begins to thicken. Stir in the salt. Remove from the heat and add the cheese and cooked pancetta or bacon, mixing well with a spoon to incorporate. Taste and adjust the seasoning.

To serve, mound the fries on a platter and pour over the blue cheese béchamel sauce. Scatter over the crumbled blue cheese and the chives. Top with the set-aside bacon slices, arranged in a criss-cross pattern. Serve immediately.

CURRY FRIES

This is a British chip-shop staple that's hugely popular. The sauce is usually a powdered mix but, when made from scratch, it does elevate this well above the average. Depending on how hot you like your curry, adjust the curry-powder heat in the recipe and if lots of chilli is desired, add a good pinch of chilli flakes as well. Great with an ice-cold beer.

Classic Fries (see page 13)

CURRY SAUCE

2 tbsp vegetable oil

1 onion, grated

1 apple, peeled and grated

1 garlic clove, crushed

2-cm/¾-inch piece of fresh ginger, peeled and grated

2 tbsp medium-hot curry powder

1 tsp turmeric

1 tsp paprika

2 tsp ground cumin

½ tsp ground coriander

1 tbsp plain/all-purpose flour

500 ml/2 cups chicken or vegetable stock

1 tsp Worcestershire sauce

1 tbsp tomato purée/paste

freshly squeezed lemon juice and/or sugar, to taste

SERVES 4

First, prepare the curry sauce. Heat the oil in a large non-stick frying pan/skillet with the onion. Cook over a medium heat, stirring occasionally, for about 3–5 minutes until aromatic.

Add the apple, garlic, ginger, curry powder, turmeric, paprika, ground cumin and ground coriander and cook, stirring for about 1 minute.

Add the flour and a splash more oil if it is very dry, and cook, stirring continuously, for another 1 minute. While stirring, gradually pour in the stock and stir until well blended. Bring just to the boil, then lower the heat to a

simmer. Stir in the Worcestershire sauce and tomato purée and simmer for 15 minutes. Taste. Depending on preference, add some lemon juice for more acidity or a pinch of sugar to sweeten, or both. Transfer the sauce to a blender and whizz until smooth. Set aside while you prepare the fries, according to the recipe for Classic Fries on page 13.

To serve, reheat the curry sauce. Mound the fries on a platter and pour over the sauce. Serve immediately.

POUTINE

Classic Fries (see page 13)

300 g/10½ oz. curd cheese, or thinly sliced halloumi

FOR THE GRAVY

1 shallot, very finely chopped

4 tbsp unsalted butter

30 g/2 tbsp plain/all-purpose flour

500 ml/2 cups beef stock, hot

500 ml/2 cups chicken stock, hot

2 tbsp tomato ketchup

1 tbsp malt vinegar

splash of Worcestershire sauce

salt and black pepper

SERVES 4

This is a Montreal classic, and it's easy to see why, if you think about the winter weather there. A portion of fries with gravy and cheese is just what you need when an icy wind blows in off the St Lawrence river. If you can't find curd cheese, halloumi will give a similar squeaky texture and mild taste, otherwise try string cheese or even cubes of Monterey Jack.

For the gravy, put the shallot and butter in a saucepan and cook over a medium heat for about 3 minutes until just soft.

Add the flour and cook, stirring constantly, for 1 minute. Add the remaining ingredients and cook, stirring, until the gravy comes to the boil. Lower the heat and continue cooking, stirring continuously, for about 5 minutes more until thick. Taste and adjust the seasoning. Set aside while you make the fries.

Prepare and cook the fries following the instructions on page 13. Reheat the gravy.

To serve, divide the fries between four bowls and then add the cheese. Pour over the hot gravy and serve immediately.

1 tbsp vegetable oil

1 small onion, finely chopped

1 small red (bell) pepper, diced

2 garlic cloves, crushed

400 g/14 oz. minced/ground beef

1 tsp ground cumin

1 tsp dried oregano

½ tsp cayenne pepper, or to taste

1 x 400-g/14-oz. can chopped tomatoes

1 x 400-g/14-oz. can black beans, drained

Classic Fries (see page 13)

Worcestershire sauce, optional

chilli/chili sauce, optional

Tabasco, optional

125 g/1¼ cups finely grated/shredded mild cheese, such as Monterey Jack or mild Cheddar

few spoonfuls of sour cream

1 spring onion/scallion, finely chopped

salt and black pepper

SERVES 4

CHILLI FRIES

This is a burger-joint classic. It is messy, substantial and not very glamorous, but boy does it taste good. This is French-fry cuisine at its finest.

In a large pot, combine the oil, onion and pepper and cook over a medium heat, stirring, until soft.

Add the garlic and meat and cook, stirring to break up the pieces, until cooked through. Add the cumin, oregano and cayenne pepper, stir well and cook for 1 minute longer.

Season well with salt and pepper and stir in the tomatoes, fill the tomato can halfway with water, stir and add it, along with the beans. Lower the heat and simmer, covered, for 20–30 minutes.

Prepare and cook the Classic Fries by following the instructions on page 13 while the chilli simmers.

Taste the chilli and adjust the seasoning, adding any sauces as desired.

To serve, mound the fries on a platter and pour over the chilli. Scatter over the cheese, dollop on the sour cream and finish with the spring onions. Serve immediately.

PEPPERONI PIZZA FRIES

Tomato sauce and melted cheese go well on a bread dough base so why not serve them atop a mound of fries? Pepperoni slices help this along very nicely, but anything that works on a pizza will work here, so do please do feel free to experiment with toppings.

Classic Fries (see page 13)

1 tbsp vegetable oil

1 red onion, halved and thinly sliced

1 tsp dried oregano

2 tbsp balsamic vinegar

200 g/7 oz. passata/ strained tomatoes

55 g/2 oz. pepperoni slices, halved if large

50 g/2 oz. stoned/pitted black olives, sliced

350 g/3 cups finely chopped or ready grated/ shredded mozzarella

SERVES 4

Prepare and cook the fries following the instructions on page 13.

Meanwhile, heat the oil and fry the onion and oregano in a small frying pan/skillet until soft. Add the balsamic vinegar and cook, stirring, until evaporated. Set aside.

Preheat the grill/broiler to high.

Spread the fries in a shallow baking dish and drizzle the passata over, then drop on blobs of the balsamic onion. Scatter over the pepperoni followed by the olives, then top all over with the mozzarella.

Place under the preheated grill for about 5 minutes until the cheese melts and just turns golden. Serve immediately.

NACHO FRIES

Salsa is one of life's little pleasures so it shouldn't just be served with tortilla chips. This is a French-fry twist on a tex-mex staple and the flavours all thrive on their new potato-based home. Try it and see.

Classic Fries (see page 13)

1 x 400-g/14-oz. can refried beans

350 g/3 cups grated/shredded Monterey Jack or mild Cheddar

1 quantity Salsa (see page 119)

1 quantity Guacamole (see page 119)

100 g/½ cup sour cream

2 spring onions/scallions, thinly sliced

3–4 tbsp sliced pickled jalapeños, or to taste

SERVES 4

Prepare and cook the fries following the instructions on page 13. Preheat the grill/broiler to high.

Warm the refried beans in a small saucepan. Consistency varies by brand, so you may need to add a splash of water to make them easier to spoon on; if they're really thick, stir in a spoonful of salsa to help thin without diluting the taste.

Spread the fries on a shallow baking sheet and top with blobs of the beans, spread to cover fairly evenly. Scatter over the cheese in an even layer.

Place under the preheated grill for about 5 minutes until the cheese melts.

Remove from the oven and top with blobs of salsa, guacamole and sour cream. Scatter over the spring onions and jalapeños and serve.

Classic Fries (see page 13)

125 g/½ cup mayo

3 tbsp Sriracha hot sauce, plus extra to serve

kimchi of your choice

50 g/¾ cup grated/shredded mild hard cheese

1 spring onion/scallion, thinly sliced

1 tsp toasted sesame seeds

a few sprigs fresh coriander/cilantro, finely chopped

BULGOGI BEEF

2 spring onions/scallions, thinly sliced

2 garlic cloves, crushed

2 tbsp sugar

1 tbsp each sesame oil and vegetable oil

1 tablespoon mirin

125 ml/½ cup soy sauce

500 g/1 lb. 2 oz. beef steak or flank, very thinly sliced

SERVES 4

KOREAN BBQ KIMCHI FRIES

This tasty topping is giving street food vibes with its fiery Korean flavours.

One day before serving, prepare the bulgogi beef. Combine all the ingredients in a bowl and toss to coat thoroughly. Transfer to a resealable plastic bag, or a shallow glass dish and cover. Refrigerate for at least 12 hours.

The day of serving, prepare the potatoes according to the recipe for Classic Fries on page 13. Keep warm in an oven set at a low temperature while you prepare the toppings.

In a small bowl, mix the mayonnaise and the Sriracha. Set aside.

For the bulgogi beef, heat a large non-stick frying pan/skillet. When hot, add the meat and marinade and cook for 3–4 minutes, stirring once or twice, until just seared.

To serve, pile the cooked fries on a platter. Scattter over the kimchi, bulgogi beef and cheese, then drizzle over the Sriracha mayo. Top with the spring onion/scallion, sesame seeds and chopped coriander/cilantro.

Serve with extra Sriracha sauce on the side.

DUTCH SATAY FRIES

Classic Fries (see page 13)

mayonnaise, for serving

1 onion, diced

SATAY SAUCE

1 tbsp peanut oil

1 small onion, grated

1 garlic clove, crushed

1-cm/½-inch piece of fresh ginger, peeled and grated

2 tsp sambal olek (Indonesian chilli/chile paste)

150 g/⅔ cup smooth peanut butter

1 tbsp soy sauce

1 tbsp clear honey or brown sugar

500 ml/2 cups chicken or vegetable stock

SERVES 4

A street food speciality of Holland, this creation pairs fries with a peanut satay sauce, mayo and diced raw onion. In Dutch it is called *pataje oorlog*, which means 'war fries'.

First, prepare the satay sauce. Heat the oil in a medium non-stick frying pan/skillet and add the grated onion. Cook over a medium heat, stirring occasionally, for 3–5 minutes until aromatic. Add the garlic, ginger and sambal olek and cook, stirring for about 30 seconds. Stir in the peanut butter, soy sauce, honey or brown sugar and stock and stir until well blended. Simmer for 3–5 minutes. If the mixture is very thick, add water or more stock to thin. Taste. Add more soy and/or honey depending on preference. Set aside while you prepare the fries.

Prepare the fries according to the recipe for Classic Fries on page 13.

To serve, gently reheat the satay sauce. Mound the fries on a platter and pour over the sauce, a few dollops of mayo and scatter over the diced onion. Serve immediately.

BBQ CHICKEN FRIES

Chicken, barbecue sauce and fries often end up together on a plate, so this combo is obvious, but it's the addition of melted cheese that elevates it to new heights. A crowd-pleaser, for sure.

Classic Fries (see page 13)

300 g/10½ oz. cooked boneless chicken meat, shredded (see Note)

250 ml/1 cup BBQ Sauce (see page 119), plus more for drizzling

300 g/3 cups grated Red Leicester, or other orange mild cheese

350 g/12 oz. cheese sauce (follow the Blue Cheese Béchamel sauce recipe on page 89, but substitute grated/shredded Cheddar for the blue cheese)

salt and black pepper

SERVES 4

Prepare and cook the fries following the instructions on page 13, but undercook slightly, as they bake again to melt the cheese.

Meanwhile, in a saucepan, combine the chicken and barbecue sauce and warm over a low heat, stirring. Taste and adjust the seasoning. Set aside and keep warm.

Warm the cheese sauce in another small saucepan. Set aside and keep warm.

Preheat the oven to 200°C/180°C fan/400°F/Gas 6. Spread the fries in a shallow baking dish. Scatter the cheese all over and return to the preheated oven for about 5 minutes to melt the cheese.

Remove from the oven and pour over the warm cheese sauce, then mound the warm chicken on top. Drizzle with extra BBQ sauce and serve.

Note: The meat from two leg and thigh portions of a large chicken is about the right amount. For the best texture, poach the chicken. Alternatively, use leftovers from a roast chicken.

PUNJABI POUTINE

A vegan and Indian twist on the Canadian classic (see page 93). The usual Canadian-style curd has an almost squeaky rubbery quality, so vegan cheese makes a great substitute with a rich butter masala-style sauce in place of the gravy.

SPICED 'CHEESE'

200 g/7 oz. Violife mozzarella-style vegan cheese

4 garlic cloves, crushed

1 tsp ground ginger

¼ tsp chilli/chili powder

¼ tsp ground turmeric

1 tsp garam masala, lightly toasted

¼ tsp salt

BUTTER MASALA GRAVY

50 ml/3½ tbsp vegetable oil or ghee

4–5 cardamom pods, crushed

5-cm/2-inch piece of cassia bark or cinnamon

4 cloves

1 large onion, finely chopped

5-cm/2-inch thumb of ginger, finely chopped

2–4 green chillies/chiles, to taste, cut lengthways

2½ tsp mild paprika

½–1 tsp chilli/chili powder, to taste

1 tsp ground coriander

1 tsp garam masala

½ tsp fenugreek powder

4 tbsp tomato purée/paste

2 tbsp agave syrup or honey

300 ml/1¼ cups water

120 ml/½ cup soy or almond cream

1 tsp salt

handful of fresh coriander/cilantro

MASALA FRIES

500 g/1 lb. 2 oz. russet, or Maris Piper or Yukon Gold potatoes, with skins on, washed

1 litre/4¼ cups sunflower oil, for deep-frying

big pinch of flaked salt

baking sheet, lightly oiled

SERVES 2–3

Preheat the oven to 200°C/180°C fan/ 400°F/Gas 6.

Cut the cheese into 1-cm/½-inch cubes. Mix together the garlic, ginger, chilli powder, turmeric, garam masala and salt in a bowl. Add the cheese, mix well and set aside for 30 minutes.

For the gravy, heat the vegetable oil in a large pan and add the cardamom, cassia bark and cloves. Gently fry until the aroma is released, then add the onion. Fry gently until the onion is transluscent and starting to turn golden. Remove the whole spices. Add the ginger, chillies, paprika, chilli powder, ground coriander, garam masala and fenugreek powder to the large pan, and fry gently for 2 minutes. Then add the tomato purée, agave syrup and water. Bring to a simmer and season to taste with salt and more syrup if needed. Simmer gently for 10–15 minutes, then add the cream. Bring back to a simmer, then remove from the heat. This sauce can simply be reheated as needed.

To make the fries, slice the potatoes into 1 cm/½ inch wide fries. Heat the oil for deep-frying in a large deep pan or wok over a medium heat. The oil needs to be hot enough for blanching on the first frying, around 140°C/280°F. Fry the fries

for 8–10 minutes, then allow to drain on paper towels. Increase the oil temperature to 180°C/ 350°F and fry the fries for a second time until golden and crispy. Drain on clean paper towels. Repeat in batches, taking care not to crowd the pan. Sprinkle the fries with salt just before serving.

Lay the marinated cheese pieces on the prepared baking sheet and bake in the preheated oven for 6–7 minutes, until gooey and softened. Fill a serving bowl with big handful of fries, pour over the masala sauce and spoon the spiced cheese over the top. Serve immediately.

BLUE CHEESE FONDUE FRIES
WITH PICKLED RED ONION RINGS

Use a mild blue cheese such as the blended cheese Cambozola, a Danish blue or Gorgonzola for this fondue-type topping. The pickled red onions are a fresh addition and work well.

1 kg/2¼ lb. Maris Piper, Yukon Gold or King Edward potatoes

2 tbsp olive oil

250 g/9 oz. Cambozola, diced

200 g/7 oz. Gruyère, grated

1 tbsp white vinegar

1 tbsp cornflour/cornstarch

1 garlic clove, crushed

1 tsp freshly chopped thyme

150 ml/⅔ cup light blonde beer

3 tbsp single/light cream

salt and black pepper

PICKLED RED ONION RINGS

125 ml/½ cup cider vinegar

30 g/2½ tbsp granulated sugar

1 tsp salt

1 red onion, thinly sliced

1 garlic clove, thinly sliced

a pinch of black or pink peppercorns

TO SERVE (OPTIONAL)

chargrilled bread

Little Gem/Boston lettuce quarters

ripe pear wedges

SERVES 6

First make the pickled onion rings. Place the vinegar, 125 ml/½ cup water, the sugar and salt in a small saucepan and bring to the boil over a low heat. Let it boil for 1 minute, then remove from the heat.

Meanwhile, place the onion, garlic and peppercorns into a sterilized 350-ml/12-oz. jar. Pour the hot pickling mixture directly over the onion and seal the jar with a vinegar-safe lid. Cool and set aside until required.

Preheat the oven to 200°C/180°C fan/400°F/Gas 6 and line a large baking sheet with baking paper.

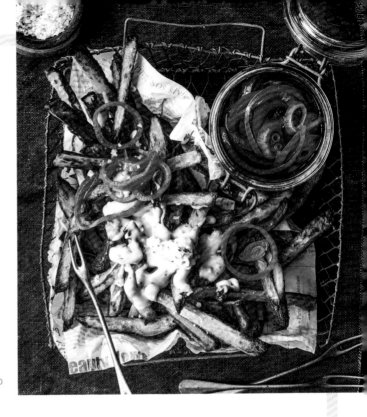

Cut the potatoes into thin fries no more than 5 mm/¼ inch thick and place on the prepared baking sheet. Add half the oil, salt and pepper and stir well. Bake in the preheated oven for 45–50 minutes, stirring from time to time, until crisp and golden.

Meanwhile, combine the cheeses with a little pepper. Stir the vinegar and cornflour together until smooth.

About 10 minutes before the potatoes are cooked, heat the remaining oil in a fondue pot or saucepan on the stovetop and gently fry the garlic and thyme over a low heat for 3 minutes until softened. Add the beer and cream and bring to the boil, then stir in the cheese until melted. Stir in the cornflour and vinegar mixture and simmer for 1–2 minutes until thickened.

Arrange the fries on plates or in bowls and spoon over the sauce. Serve with the pickled onions and chargrilled bread. Or alternatively, serve as a fondue with the fries, pickles, lettuce and pears.

5
SAUCES, DIPS & PICKLES

TOMATO KETCHUP

A trio of ketchups perfect for all fries.

1 kg/2¼ lb. ripe tomatoes, cored and chopped

150 ml/½ cup plus 2 tbsp vinegar (malt or cider)

50 g/¼ cup soft dark brown sugar

½ tsp fine salt

pinch of ground cinnamon

pinch of ground cloves

pinch of celery salt

MAKES ABOUT 500 ML/2 CUPS

Put the tomatoes in a saucepan and cook over medium-high heat, stirring occasionally, for 15–20 minutes until they break down. Transfer to a food processor and whizz until smooth, then rub through a fine-mesh sieve/strainer and return the paste to a clean pan. Continue cooking the tomato pulp over a low heat, stirring often, until very thick. Stir in the remaining ingredients and simmer for 5 minutes. Adjust the seasoning, adding more vinegar and/or sugar to taste. The sauce will keep, covered, in the fridge for at least 1 week.

CURRY KETCHUP

1 small onion, grated
2 tbsp vegetable oil
2 tbsp curry powder
1 tbsp hot paprika
½ tsp mustard powder
pinch of ground cloves
500 g/generous 2 cups. passata/
strained tomatoes
6 tbsp dark brown sugar
125 ml/½ cup malt vinegar
salt

MAKES ABOUT 400 ML/1⅔ CUPS

In a saucepan, soften the onion in
the oil, 3–5 minutes. Stir in all the
spices and cook until aromatic,
about 1 minute more. Add the
passata, sugar, vinegar and salt to
taste. Stir to dissolve and bring to
the boil, then lower the heat and
simmer until thick like ketchup.
Taste and adjust seasoning. The
sauce will keep, covered, in the
fridge for at least 1 week.

CHILLI KETCHUP

1 small onion, finely chopped
1 tbsp vegetable oil
1 garlic clove, crushed
700 g/scant 3 cups passata/
strained tomatoes
¼ tsp chilli/hot red pepper
flakes
1 tsp tomato ketchup
splash of cider vinegar
salt and black pepper

MAKES ABOUT 500 ML/2 CUPS

In a saucepan, soften the onion
in the oil, 3–5 minutes. Stir in the
garlic, passata, chilli flakes and
ketchup and bring to the boil, then
lower the heat and simmer until
thick. Add some salt, pepper and a
splash of vinegar; taste and adjust
seasoning. It will keep, covered, in
the fridge for at least 1 week.

KALUA CHIPOTLE KETCHUP

This Mexican-inspired sauce has everything you want with heat and a deep smoky undertone.

3 x 400-g/14-oz. cans whole Italian tomatoes
3 tbsp dark soy sauce
3 tbsp muscovado sugar
1 tsp fish sauce
1 tbsp mirin
3 tbsp chipotle paste

MAKES ABOUT 600 ML/2½ CUPS

Put the whole tomatoes in a saucepan and heat gently. Add the soy sauce, muscovado sugar, fish sauce and mirin. Stir and bring the mixture to a very low simmer. Add in the chipotle paste and stir together. Continue to simmer for about 30 minutes until slightly reduced. Then put everything in a blender and whizz to a smooth purée.

Pour the warm sauce into sterilized bottles or jars and seal. Store in a dry place, out of the light. Once open, keep the bottle in the fridge and use within 1 week.

CHIPOTLE CREMA

A creamy, milder version of the chipotle ketchup, this one works on anything.

1 tbsp Kalua Chipotle Ketchup (see left) or chipotle paste
3 tbsp double/heavy cream
1 tbsp good-quality mayonnaise

MAKES 5 TBSP

Mix the ingredients together in a bowl.

ROAST GARLIC & CHIPOTLE MAYO

This lovely mayonnaise is really big on flavour and very versatile.

2 large garlic cloves, skin on
4 tbsp mayonnaise
½ tsp crushed Chipotle chilli/chile

MAKES 4 TBSP

Preheat the oven to 180°C/160°C fan/350°F/Gas 4.

Roast the garlic on a baking sheet in the preheated oven for 20 minutes until soft but not burnt. Remove from the oven and let cool for 10 minutes.

Squeeze the garlic from its skin into a small bowl. Gently mash with a fork. Add the mayonnaise and Chipotle and stir until evenly mixed. Cover and refrigerate for 2–3 hours to let the Chipotle rehydrate a little in the mayonnaise. Stir occasionally while it's chilling.

FRESH AIOLI

This is an all-time classic dip, brilliant with fries, anything potato-related or barbecue food. This recipe has a wonderful robust garlicky flavour.

2 large egg yolks
4 very fresh garlic cloves, crushed
1 tsp Dijon mustard
150 ml/⅔ cup good-quality light olive oil
freshly squeezed juice of ½ lemon
salt and black pepper

MAKES ABOUT 150 ML/⅔ CUP

Beat the egg yolks in a large bowl with a balloon whisk. Add the garlic and mustard and beat through. While beating the mixture, slowly add the olive oil in a thin, steady stream. When all the oil has been added, the aioli should have a smooth, velvety appearance. Add the lemon juice, season with salt and pepper and gently stir through. Refrigerate until needed.

GREEN GODDESS MAYO

A trio of creamy mayos for dipping.

200 g/¾ cup plus 2 tbsp mayonnaise

50 ml/3 tbsp sour cream

freshly squeezed juice of ½ lemon

2–3 anchovy fillets, finely chopped

small bunch chives, finely chopped

2 sprigs each fresh tarragon, parsley and basil, leaves finely chopped

1 tbsp capers in brine, drained and finely chopped

1 small garlic clove, crushed

Tabasco, optional

salt and black pepper

MAKES 250 ML/1 CUP

Combine all the ingredients in a bowl and stir well to blend. Taste and adjust seasoning. Let stand at least 30 minutes before serving.

CHILLI & LIME GARLIC MAYO

250 g/1 cup plus 2 tbsp mayonnaise

2 garlic cloves, crushed

½ fresh red chilli/chile, deseeded and finely chopped

zest and freshly squeezed juice of 1 lime

MAKES 250 ML/1 CUP

Combine all the ingredients in a bowl and mix well. Let stand at least 30 minutes before serving.

TRUFFLE MAYO

250 g/1 cup plus 1 tbsp fresh mayonnaise

1 tbsp truffle oil

a few chives, very finely chopped

truffle salt, to taste

MAKES 250 ML/1 CUP

Combine the mayonnaise, oil and chives in a bowl and mix well. Let stand at least 30 minutes before serving. Just before serving, dust with a good pinch of truffle salt.

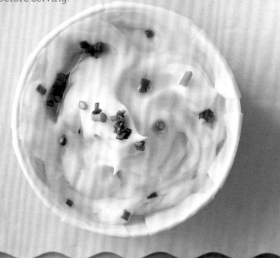

BBQ SAUCE

A classic sauce for serving with fries.

500 ml/2 cups tomato ketchup
60 ml/¼ cup malt vinegar
60 ml/¼ cup Worcestershire sauce
50 g/¼ cup dark brown sugar
2 tbsp clear honey
2 tbsp mustard powder
¼ tsp paprika
¼ tsp ground cumin
¼ tsp garlic powder
generous pinch chilli/hot red pepper flakes

MAKES 600 ML/2½ CUPS

Combine all the ingredients in a saucepan and bring just to the boil over a medium heat. Reduce the heat to low and simmer for 15 minutes. Taste and adjust the seasoning, adding more salt, vinegar or chilli flakes to taste. The sauce will keep, covered, in the refrigerator for at least 1 week.

GUACAMOLE

This Mexican dip works perfectly as a tasty topping for loaded fries.

2 ripe avocados, pitted and mashed
3–4 tbsp sour cream
freshly squeezed juice of ½ lemon
small bunch fresh coriander/cilantro, finely chopped
pinch of ground cumin
½ tsp fine sea salt
1 small fresh red chilli/chile, finely chopped, optional

SERVES 4

Combine all the ingredients in a bowl and mix well. Taste and adjust seasoning, adding more salt or lemon juice as desired. Serve at once.

SALSA

A fresh and tangy salsa for dipping or topping.

2 fresh green jalapeños
400-g/14-oz. can plum tomatoes
small bunch fresh coriander/cilantro, trimmed
1 small onion, coarsely chopped
1 garlic clove, crushed
good pinch ground cumin
pinch of salt and sugar
freshly squeezed juice of ½ lime

SERVES 4

Preheat the oven to 200°C/180°C fan/400°F/Gas 6. Roast the jalapeños for 15–20 minutes until tender. Let cool. Remove the seeds.

Put all the ingredients in a food processor and whizz until smooth. Transfer to a bowl and taste for seasoning. Let stand for 30 minutes before serving. It will keep, covered, in the refrigerator for at least 5 days.

HARISSA, YOGURT & LEMON DIP

A tangy dip to pair well with strong flavours.

200 g/7 oz. Greek yogurt
1 tsp harissa paste
¼ preserved lemon, rind only, finely chopped
pinch of sumac
clear honey, for drizzling

SERVES 4

Combine the yogurt, harissa and lemon rind in a bowl and stir to blend. Sprinkle over the sumac and top with a few swirls of honey. Serve.

BEETROOT, YOGURT & MINT DIP

This vibrant dip looks beautiful on the plate.

400 g/14 oz. cooked beet(root)
2 tbsp extra virgin olive oil
6–8 tbsp Greek yogurt
2 garlic cloves, crushed
pinch of ground cumin
few fresh mint leaves, finely chopped
salt and black pepper

SERVES 4–6

In a food processor, combine the beetroot, oil and yogurt and whizz to obtain a coarse dip. Transfer to a bowl and stir in the garlic, cumin and a pinch of salt. Taste and adjust seasoning. Sprinkle with the mint and serve.

LEMON & TAHINI DIP

A moreish dip to add to any meal.

200 g/7 oz. Greek yogurt
3 tbsp tahini
1 garlic clove, crushed
freshly squeezed juice of ½ lemon
1 spring onion/scallion, finely chopped
1 tsp toasted sesame seeds
clear honey, for drizzling
pomegranate molasses, for drizzling

SERVES 4

In a bowl, stir together the yogurt, tahini, garlic, lemon juice and spring onion. Sprinkle over the sesame seeds and top with a drizzle of honey, followed by a drizzle of pomegranate molasses. Serve.

SPICY DILL PICKLES

A trio of crunchy pickles that work perfectly as a side to fries.

1 litre/4 cups water

300 ml/1¼ cups white vinegar

3 tbsp sea salt

8 dill sprigs

8 large garlic cloves

4 dried hot chilli/ chile peppers

675 g/24 oz. pickling cucumbers, quartered or halved and sliced lengthwise

4 x sterilized 450 ml/16 oz. canning jars

MAKES 4 JARS

In a stainless steel stockpot, bring the water, vinegar and salt to the boil. Let boil for about 10–12 minutes.

Meanwhile, pack the cucumbers facing upwards into canning jars. Make sure they are at least 1.25 cm/½ inch below the jar's rim. Place 2 dill sprigs, 2 garlic cloves and 1 chilli pepper in each jar. Carefully ladle the hot mixture into the jars. Add extra water if necessary so that the cucumbers are submerged, but leave 1.25 cm/½ inch of space from the rim of the jar. Remove air bubbles, wipe the rims and put the lids on. Let the cucumbers pickle for at least 24 hours before tasting.

SWEET PICKLES

240 ml/1 cup cider vinegar

40 g/⅛ cup salt

200 g/1 cup granulated sugar

¼ tsp ground turmeric

½ tsp mustard seed

400 g/14 oz. pickling cucumbers, quartered or halved and sliced lengthwise

1 sweet onion, sliced

2 x sterilized 450 ml/16 oz. canning jars

MAKES 2 JARS

In a small saucepan over a medium-high heat, combine the cider vinegar, salt, sugar, turmeric and mustard seed. Bring to the boil and let cook for 5 minutes.

Loosely pack the cucumbers and the onion into canning jars and pour the hot liquid over them. Remove air bubbles, wipe the rims and put the lids on. Let the cucumbers pickle for at least 24 hours before tasting.

SWEET & SOUR CHERRY PICKLES

½ jar Spicy Dill Pickles (see left), including the brine

1 packet cherry Kool-Aid powder

200 g/1 cup granulated sugar

1 x sterilized 450 ml/16 oz. canning jar

MAKES 1 JAR

Follow the recipe to the left for spicy dill pickles. After the brining is done, remove the pickles from the liquid. Stir in the sugar and the Kool-Aid to the pickle brine until they have both dissolved. Add the pickles back to the mixture, and seal in the jar. Place in the refrigerator and let brine for at least 1 week before tasting.

SALTED HERBES DE PROVENCE

A perfect herby salt to sprinkle over crispy fries.

2 tbsp dried thyme

2 tsp dried rosemary

2 tsp dried basil

2 tsp fennel seeds

2 tsp dried sage

2 tsp sea salt flakes

3 tbsp dried lavender flowers

MAKES 85 G/3 OZ

Mix all the ingredients in a bowl, then store in a glass jar for up to 6 months.

SMOKY AFRICAN RUB

This is a simple sprinkle for fries laced with smoked salt, giving them a hearty bite.

1 tsp smoked sea salt

1 tsp coarse-ground garlic powder

1 tsp ground black pepper

1 tbsp dried chilli flakes/hot red pepper flakes

1 tsp fenugreek seeds

2 dried bay leaves

MAKES 3 TBSP

Put all the ingredients into an electric spice grinder and process to a coarse powder.

Store the spice mix in a glass jar with a tight-fitting lid for up to 6 months.

DUKKAH

Traditionally you would dip a piece of bread into olive oil and then into this Egyptian dip, but it works equally well with crispy fries or sprinkled on the Aubergine & Sumac Fries on page 43.

40g/1½ oz. each hazelnuts, fennel seeds, cumin seeds and coriander seeds
80g/generous ½ cup sesame seeds
1 tsp sel gris
½ tsp cracked black pepper

MAKES 300 G/10½ OZ

In a hot pan, toast the hazelnuts and each of the spices separately. Leave to cool slightly then put all the ingredients in a food processor and pulse a few times.

CAJUN SPICED SALT

Cajun seasonings are a wonderful addition to any kind of meat, fish, poultry or vegetable dish, and work perfectly when used as a spicy seasoning for fries.

2 tsp ground cumin
2 tsp cayenne pepper
2 tbsp Spanish smoked paprika (pimentòn)
2 tsp dried thyme
2 tsp dried oregano
1 tsp dried garlic powder
2 tsp turbinado/demerara sugar
1 tsp sea salt
1 tsp ground black pepper

MAKES 6½ TBSP/SCANT ½ CUP

Put all the ingredients in a bowl and mix together. Store the salt in a glass jar with a tight-fitting lid for up to 6 months.

INDEX

RECIPE CREDITS

Valerie Aikman-Smith
Cajun Spiced Salt
Dukkah
Salted Herbes de
  Provence
Smoky African Rub

Julz Beresford
Manchego Cheese Balls

Megan Davies
Lemon & Pecorino
  Polenta Fries
Baked Potato Skins with
  Butter
Potato Peel Chips

**Felipe Fuentes Cruz &
Ben Fordham**
Beer-battered Avocado
  Dippers

Carol Hilker
Ale-battered Onion
  Rings
Deep-fried Mozzarella
  Sticks
Fried Green Tomatoes
Paprika & Chilli Fries
Spicy Dill Pickles
Sweet Pickles
Sweet & Sour Cherry
  Pickles
Tater Tots

Jackie Kearney
Baked Vegan Aubergine
  Fries
Beer-battered Pickles
Indonesian Corn 'Ribs'
Punjabi Poutine

Jenny Linford
Piquant Potato Straws
Triple-cooked Chips

Dan May
Fresh Aioli
Roast Garlic & Chipotle
  Mayo

Louise Pickford
Blue Cheese Fondue
Loaded Fries

James Porter
Chipotle Crema
Kalua Chipotle Ketchup

Annie Rigg
Patatas Bravas

Chef Tee
Green Plantain Fritters
Plantain Wedges
Sweet Potato Fries

Jenny Tschiesche
Bocconcini Balls
Crispy Courgette Fries
Cumin Carrot Fries
Herby Swede Fries

**Laura Washburn
Hutton**
Aubergine & Sumac Fries
Avocado Fries with Sour
  Cream Dip
BBQ Chicken Fries
BBQ Sauce
Beetroot, Yogurt & Mint
  Dip
Blue Cheese & Bacon
  Fries
Chilli & Lime Garlic
  Mayo
Chilli Fries
Chilli Ketchup
Classic Fries
Curry Fries
Curry Ketchup

Dutch Satay Fries
Garlic & Herb Potato
  Wedges with Garlic
  Lemon Mayo
Green Goddess
Guacamole
Halloumi & Za'atar Fries
Harissa, Yogurt & Lemon
  Dip
Korean BBQ Kimchi Fries
Lemon-Pepper
  Asparagus Fries with
  Lemon Dip
Lemon & Tahini Dip
Matchstick Fries with
  Sichuan Pepper Salt
Nacho Fries
Oven-baked Beetroot
  Fries with Wasabi
  Mayo
Oven-baked Celeriac
  Fries with Honey &
  Thyme
Pepperoni Pizza Fries
Polenta & Parmesan
  Parsnip Fries
Poutine
Rustic Steak Fries
Salsa
Sweetcorn-Sage Polenta
  Fries
Tomato Ketchup
Truffle Fries
Truffle Mayo

PHOTOGRAPHY CREDITS

Steve Baxter
Pages 30 and 84.

Peter Cassidy
Pages 19, 65, 69 and 123.

Steve Painter
Pages 1, 2, 3, 5, 6, 9, 10, 13,
14, 16, 20, 23, 34, 37, 42,
46, 52, 57, 58, 61, 62, 88,
91, 92, 95, 96, 99, 100, 103,
104, 110, 112–113, 116–117,
118 and 120–121.

Rita Platts
Pages 54, 72 and 73.

Toby Scott
Pages 66, 70 and 80.

Ian Wallace
Pages 86 and 109.

Clare Winfield
Pages 24, 27, 28, 32, 38,
41, 45, 49, 50, 75, 76, 79,
83 and 107.